We Have Seen the Corn

We Have Seen the Corn

Poems by

Stephanie L. Harper

© 2025 Stephanie L. Harper. All rights reserved.
This material may not be reproduced in any form, published,
reprinted, recorded, performed, broadcast,
rewritten or redistributed without
the explicit permission of Stephanie L. Harper.
All such actions are strictly prohibited by law.

Cover design by Shay Culligan
Cover image "Conspiring Skyward" by Cameren Harper
Author photo by Robert Okaji

ISBN: 978-1-63980-761-1

Kelsay Books
502 South 1040 East, A-119
American Fork, Utah 84003
Kelsaybooks.com

For Bob: My One

Acknowledgements

With gratitude to the editors of the following journals for publishing poems (often in earlier versions):

The Big Windows Review: "Winter Poem"
Caesura: "The Hole"
Cathexis Northwest Press: "Aubade with Smoke"
The Dodge: "By the Moonlit Water Where the *Dombiki* Sing"
Dust Poetry Magazine: "Trace"
Five South: "Dear Autocorrect"
Foothill Journal: "(Cento) I'm tired of understanding . . ."
formidable woman sanctuary: "Glory Be . . ."
The Iowa Review: "Pelvic Organ Prolapse"
Months to Years: "The Corpus Callosum Is Unremarkable"
Narrative Northeast: "The Chickens"
Panoply: "Reporting Live from the Hornet's Nest"
Parcham Magazine: "Letter from the Other Side of Silence"
Rat's Ass Review: "Of These One and All"
Resurrection Magazine: "Indigo Bunting," "Child's Pose," "Gateway"
Riggwelter Press: "We Have Seen the Corn"
Rough Diamond Poetry Journal: "Baby Robins"
Salamander Magazine: "(Cento) Presentiment"
Samjoko Magazine: "Sestina for a Queen: Northern Cardinal"
Slippery Elm Literary Journal: "Answer"
Taos Poetry Journal: "The Final Frontier"

Contents

Indigo Bunting	11
Answer	12
(Cento) I'm tired of understanding . . .	14
The Hole	15
Pelvic Organ Prolapse	17
Ghazal of the Slumbering Entomophile	19
Reporting Live from the Hornet's Nest	20
Sestina for a Queen: Northern Cardinal	21
The Chickens	23
Aubade with Smoke	24
Letter from the Other Side of Silence	25
We Have Seen the Corn	26
Gateway	28
Trace	29
Glory Be . . .	30
Dear Autocorrect	31
Of These One and All	32
Winter Poem	33
Child's Pose	35
Note on the Discovery of the *Real* Lake Wobegon	37
(Cento) Presentiment	38
The Corpus Callosum Is Unremarkable	39
Ghazal sans Answers	40
How to Squeeze Blood from a Turnip	41
Baby Robins	43
The Final Frontier	45
By the Moonlit Water Where the *Dombiki* Sing	47
Notes	49

Indigo Bunting

innermost   & most

neophyte-like   are these

discords

i   still

grieve—   *& yet   this*

opalescence   dawning

blue—

unbridled wings

nasturtium-blooms   &

topaz skies—

is   my Indiana

never nigher to

grace

Answer

How did the womb's hush, little goat,
        groom your aptitude to bleat so
& sidle your silken haunches up to me?

The way you press your distended
        pintsized abdomen against my knee
& butt my outstretched hand with your horn buds,
        begging for the sun-ripe shoots
along the far side of the fence,
        brings me to a robust belief in need.

O, babe, no, I won't leave you
before the cricket-song's lull is in full-swing,
        though, the dusk is rushing in
to replace afternoon's haze
        & twilight would usher me to the dark
of another sleep weeping like the moon
engorged above the sagebrush-muddled hills . . .

        Last night, in a dream of my children
        when they were still young,
        there was neither time nor help enough
        to feed their many (all-too-realistic) demands—
            from the toting of their two pajamaed bodies
        to the car to park them in a driveway four houses away
        (at the crux of their convoluted breakfast ritual),
        to rejections, in equal parts irrational & resolute,
        of the given dream-morning's cereal offerings . . .

What mother doesn't dream of baby goats?
Hear their cries in her mind & answer
        in harmonic bleats?
Hunger for sweet greens, just out of reach?
Bed down in warm hay beneath the starlight
        bleeding through the barn's worm-worn roof?

(Cento) I'm tired of understanding . . .

morning. *Why and why and why* bleeds slowly
from my mouth at the brown brink generations
have trod and trod and trod, the sparse bright
sprinkle of grass burnishing over into the
universe of shimmer. It is hard to remain
human, drawn from the cold, hard mouth
of the world the moths have visited. At mid-
summer, the gnats were here to be together,
selfless, all, all for all, utterly free. When birds
perch weeping in the trees before the dawn,
an orange light returns to the mountains: if you
tasted it, it would first taste bitter, then briny,
then surely burn the beginnings of your breaths.
Oh, what shall I say, how is the truth to be said?

Credits: Lucille Clifton, Gerard Manley Hopkins, Elizabeth Bishop, Charles Wright, Mark Doty, D. A. Powell, W. S. Merwin, Gwendolyn Brooks

The Hole

twinge
above your right brow

in a mirror   that dusky spot

the hole
acute   scalene   deep
about an inch in height
just above your right eyeball
loosened from its socket
oozing blood
from cracks around your lids

a clear view
to the back of your skull—
the bone is floodlit like a surgical theater

accentuating the osseous fabric's
orderly interweaving of dark
green lettuce leaves
with your head's sealed fissures

it makes no sense
but to accept it—

your neighbor   who constantly drops by
unannounced   needs you   again
to watch her kids tomorrow afternoon
"for just a few hours"

sure   not a problem

she'll be inviting you to her wedding this summer
"third time's the charm"

how nice

a flash
on the porcelain screen
(where your brain should be)
previews the upcoming afternoon—

gazebo with picnic tables
at the breezy confluence
of the Columbia & Willamette rivers

daylight encasing you in the naked
mole-rat's skin you'd mistaken
for a modest-pink sundress

siphoning the cash bar's cut-rate Riesling
as you try to make small-talk without thinking

about the cool tingle of exposed bone
above your right brow
flora   slick in plasma   creeping out—

which puts extra strain on the wobbly eyeball . . .

Pelvic Organ Prolapse

—An In-titled Poem

A pop?

No, no gore, per se—
no large rip in one snap;
no *real* pain;
no slop, no slip, nor special pose governs—
save one   long   sag | a sparse *oops* elapsing once, again . . .

A plain ol' organic lapse in core,
or lag in poise, reaping a gape;
is loose; is an evil viper, alive, sere,
roving over a polar sea, sparing no salve,
no caring, no clear love—
is no pal;   leaves one cooling in one's pee . . .

Is a page in lore:

As one ages, one earns one's pro role (give props!) as a vaginal
    pagan

sieve;   is a *proper* lap, as graven icons go::envisage an opal rose
    in a pleasing vale, lips
seeping rain;
i rinse crisp, green apples clean,
or ripen pears,
even oranges . . .

    See?   Appealing, no?

Please clap!

Please!

Please, can i grieve?

Ghazal of the Slumbering Entomophile

Does yonder chanson vibrating in the lilac tree
portend tymbals *instigating* in the lilac tree?

Sleep supplied her with an ample head of steam
to fuel such inklings of X-rating in the lilac tree . . .

In the blossoms' musky midst, the she-cicada's wingtips
clicked with ovipositor's pulsating in the lilac tree.

Le monsieur set to his amorous pursuit—
the game afoot was *dating* in the lilac tree!

How their red & beady eye-pairs, each to each,
laser-beamed designs for mating in the lilac tree!

What that burning moment left unsaid left one
two-backed beast recuperating in the lilac tree.

Then belle & beau both slunk into the leaves.
They'd quite finished copulating in the lilac tree.

And in the blooms' blue's swift receding: two stiff sheaths
still clinging to Steph's dream abating in the lilac tree . . .

Reporting Live from the Hornet's Nest

It's not like i believe refraining
from uttering the words
could make them less true—

in my limbs
they are the summer breeze
that thrills the ancient live oak's
company of competing elbows:

such is my aching
to give my breath
to this voice of *cannot*—

this unseen murmuring,
spinning silence
the golden orb spider glistens
in the dawn's sun-tinged tears.

Silk-bound wingless,
trembling, i am

the notion of a self
inhabited too briefly—

suspended—

yet, if i were to unhinge,

o, how i would
insinuate you whole

into my serpentine throat.

Sestina for a Queen: Northern Cardinal

Beaking black oil sunflower seeds, you face
down a dry leaf that slips in on the wind,
a warning the juncos heed . . . There's wildfire
alight in your eyes, as you steal sidelong
glimpses of your red-feathered swain. Your tail
fans toward his catcalls to snub, out-of-hand,

his display of early-March ardor—its hand
in your glee aside, his black, baffled face
is just too sweet . . . That's it, give him a tail
ruffle to lift his spirits—let the wind
bare your pheromones' warm truth: you belong
to him. Sunbeams in your fuzzy crest's fire

incite more songs. Each crimson glint of fire
shimmying in your wingtips has a hand
in his vigor to dig in for the long
frozen weeks till spring again shows her face
(seeking the north's greener prospects) to wind
her balmy way in from the Gulf & dovetail

with daylight's surge burgeoning fat cattail
reeds in culverts abloom with bergamot fire.
Nesting in the white pine, safe from the wind,
you'll find out Romeo's fortes first-hand:
When your frantic hatchlings beg will he face
his fatherly onus with grace, or long

for bachelorhood? Any bets on how long
he'll keep up the ruse when the fledglings tail
him everywhere? Will he shun that blameless face
of your one cowbird chick who eats like fire

in a dry gulch in August? Watch him hand
off foraging lessons as soon as the wind

kicks up June's first thunderstorm . . . You could wind
up an old brooding hen before the long
days start to wane . . . Oh, but you've got to hand
it to those kisses of his—   no detail
missed, not a seed-heart left unstripped! What fire
his coral-beaked pecks blaze across your face!

Though the wind sets your tail-plumes a flutter
as his wooing stokes your long-burning fire,
a queen's face shall speak for your handmaid's heart.

The Chickens

So much about baking
blackberry muffins

on a fall afternoon
depends upon thoughts

of your neighbor's bantam rooster
Hamlet

& his tawny sister
Nugget

oh   those tiny dinosaurs
with blue feet!

how they strut alongside
the road

uncrossed   & sleekening
in the low sun's gold

Aubade with Smoke

That i left my window open
last night & let in wildfire smoke

as i drifted off to Katydids lullabying
in the waxing crescent's red haze

explains my waking this morning
to teary eyes   a husky throat

limbs heavy with sleep's intoxication
& the strange orange of smoldering rays

but not my drowning—

no. For *this* i blame
the dream i composed
to get you alone
& let the flood come—
o!—   how its pulsing
reproof   *Don't!* ...   *Don't!* ...
so heartlessly
bore me away from you   ...

Now   as i rise to the surface—

to the day-lit breeze already revived
& stoking its hot defiance

of yesterday's firelines—

with your name seared on my lips

i am ablaze . . .

Letter from the Other Side of Silence

Dear One: A life-long dusk of onyx-black
has failed to send back even faint echoes
of my own refrains. I know what it is
to be mocked by the night-wind's naked hiss
in the surf's stultifying reprise:
*This something-other-than-living is all
there is* . . .
But now that our *Unsaying* has sprouted
to the surface, basked in summer light &
given over its once-crucial husk to
the fallow soil's renewal, what is left
for it but to inhabit its belly & sing
from its deep . . . ?
Warbling wildly between the future's
topographies & the past's veiled griefs—
its crystal vibrato proclaiming:
Yours is to live!—
my mind registers such magic as would teach
the sea-floor's stones to rise up & stitch closed
our world's most ancient of gulfs . . .
This distance, with its plane of coordinates
made-up to separate us, has no bearing
on our shared heart's magnetic north—
so, it's no wonder that I hear your voice
as clearly & close to the core of Truth
as my own, for we are of the same string-stuff:
elements with which I've already composed
more terms of affection for you than I dreamed
I'd ever know! You are *The Speaking*, itself;
& I, no longer a wraith, am *body & breath*
who will live the rest of my days learning
to say your name . . .

We Have Seen the Corn

with twelve-hundred miles
of fields in our wake

I am aching
to slip among those stalks & touch

their silk-topped ears all conspiring
skyward now

to beguile the birds' cries from the brim
of that thundercloud

burgeoning
over the Nebraska plain

let's pull off the interstate   so we can
stretch our legs for a bit

Indiana will wait

split those crows' itinerant
congregation   there   & park

right alongside the unending green
I want to enter

its late-sun-streams sifting the sky motes
crimson-gold   & stirring

the cicadas' whirrs & earwigs' scuttles in the loam
to a viscous chorus

& with my hand clasped in yours   press
another lush measure

into our song's sweet & sultry folds

Gateway

they keep it a secret
to stop you
but when you find it
you'll step through . . .
one   taste
in this far-away place of
flourless chocolate cake
of no more bran clusters or
Brussel's sprouts shoulding you
no more stale crusts demanding
Who do you think you are?
now   you'll be forever
enraptured by the devil's food
in the universe of YOU:
oh yes!   all of you!
your sweeps & furrows!
your savors unfurled
to his reverent tongue
his warmth ushering you
quiver by undulant quiver
into the deep-delicious
coalescence that is
The   Chocolate   Cake
of a woman   unbound

marveling   *how?*

how is it that I'm not yet full?

how is it that I'm still alive?

Trace

—For Bob on our Wedding Day

In your morning boule & black coffee,
or mélange of pancetta with eggs;
in your countertop crumbs & unsolidified
splatters sponged-up & sink-bound;

in Pandora's box of Edgar Meyer phenotypes
unseating the disquietude of our former lives;
in your afternoon *cappuccino* you pronounce in Italian
& in your full belly's tranquil cogitations;

in your evening removal of socks & your feet's relief;
& in your crescent smile's light sheltering me—
as my kisses press away the decades' trace

of borne iniquities from your handsome face
on their way to the dimple of your left cheek—
is *everywhere* my home will be.

Glory Be . . .

to my husband's exquisite
nipples—a cactus-hen's chicks
snug in black silk vortices—
two galactic fornices
abloom in silver spacetime,
cresting, ruddy, from the rime.
Glory be to his two, cute
accretion discs—each hirsute
sentry perched in its crow's nest,
a bold basilisk, abreast
of his heartbeats' *whole* ocean—
keeping the time dilation
lanterns burning damask-rose:
Leading where? *Oh! Glory knows* . . .

Dear Autocorrect

Thank you for your patience
& support in my kite. I rely on
your spelling sand predictive
text features many things easy day.
If I couldn't trust you to witch
my typing, I would be more honest
about the tunes when I'm in
the bathroom. I bean, really,
the pastime I need is for people
to judge me because of where
I might be fitting if all I'm frying
to do is confirm the tune of our
nest nerding . . . A few fats ado,
my husband texted me from
the hardest store to ask if I could
use any more bridges for fainting
in the bedroom. Nob makes almond
anything come acrylic as romantic,
so things started jesting up a bit.
Lettuce nut say it was with all
your extra kelp that I was doom
scrolling his pencil, so he had to
duck behind a dorkloft parked by
the election law tools. It was the mist
excrement wither of us remembered
having since I went shipping last
Christmas for a new wonton hacker . . .
Anyway, I thought I'd pet you now
how much your rusty cervix beans
to me. Your fiend, Symphony.

Of These One and All

And of these one and all I weave the song of myself.
—Walt Whitman, "Song of Myself" 15

The left flesh-melon harbors a pool of sweat;
the right flesh-melon harbors a pool of sweat.

The perimenopausal woman hot-flashes in the kitchen,
while the young-adult son dons wool slippers in the kitchen.

The second husband purchases electric socks
for his perimenopausal wife.
The ex-husband, meanwhile, dissociates further
from his ex-wife . . .

And these stoke my hankering for donuts,
and I don't appreciate how lucky I am to be forced
to make do with home-baked banana-nut muffins.

And such as it is to amass five decades of knowledge—
minus where I last left my phone, that is—
I am, more or less, pressing it to my left ear and speaking on it,
as I hot-flash in the kitchen.

And of these spates of steaminess, cantankerous joints,
and suddenly uncloseable pants, one and all, I orchestrate
the opus of my middle-age . . .

Winter Poem

—For Matthew

Another Indiana winter
sets down its brown sentence;

      its barred owl hovering
over this cornfield's scoria—

      a story of things fallen
prey to the talons of cold
punctuated chalk-white
with naked sycamores:

The giant silver maple's orphaned hands
amass on the backyard deck;
the pin oak's fists clench
in brown protest.

December's subdued rays reach
through the windows; their orange suggestion
of warmth stippling the living room
is yet another of winter's ruses
condemning

      your beloved Oregon's evergreen
to memory's rearview . . .

Here, in Indiana,
even the cat's shed whisker,
a once-white shaft now absorbed
into the office desk's walnut veneer,
is a casualty of this annual assault,
left brownly inert

      when the illusory-tropical summer
you'd been savoring vanished.

My son, what weighs on you I wear
around my trunk like the husk of a dormant oak
& grow older in my latency as I weather
your browner seasons.

I know it wasn't for my sake
that you just passed the day's failing light online,
enrapt in looping time-lapses of a solar flare
on NASA's website,

      to defy the brown in your mind
with a new winter paradigm—

      of charged particles' earthward-careening
promise to ignite the thermosphere purple-green
before the oncoming front of December's first snow—

      but, oh, how seeing you
find your way aloft in this long night
of things prey to falling

                          has lifted me

Child's Pose

Inhale the distillate of night,
its sock-fuzz, cat dander & dust mites
among the carpet fibers
& exhale the walrus, the whale,
the giraffe & the three pterodactyls
exiting
through the door in your back.

Inhale the spores newly moldered
during this afternoon's warmth
now re-icing in the needles
beneath the eastern white pine
outside the media-room window
in a shaft of moonlight;
exhale the alligator
from the swamp in the Muppet Movie
stalking Dom DeLuise who's bantering
with Kermit about making millions
of people happy in Hollywood
before exiting
through the door in your back.

Inhale the essence
of your husband's baking Irish soda bread
& exhale Kermit plunking his banjo,
exhale his song about rainbows,
the rusty Schwinn he rides to the El Sleezo,
that giant pair of cartoon frog's legs erected on the roadside,
yes, exhale, exhale with your most diligent eight-count
the freshly steamrolled pavement's glisten
exiting now
through the flung-wide door in the small of your back.

Then, with the heavy-lidded inhalation that comes
just after your rump finds its final millimeter of declivity
no one had imagined,
take in affectatious Miss Piggy
winning the county fair beauty contest,
stealing the heart of a certain amphibian
& being flippant in French under a broad, starry, desert sky,
along with everything else that's trying
to enter
through the door in your back—

Note on the Discovery of the *Real* Lake Wobegon

Per a new study appearing
in the spring 2024 issue
of *Human Evolutionary
Endocrine Dysfunction*—
the quarterly publication
to which scientists with
an instinct for self-preservation
colloquially refer as *HEED:*

In a topographic model
painstakingly reconstructed
from the unassailable litany
of geologic signposts pointing
to the extant-in-perpetuity
Menopausozoic Era, intrepid
paleontologists claim to have
located this famed, palpably
undying & brackish geothermal
basin to within zero-point-three
microns in a chasm beneath two
notably dense sedimentary deposits
at: fifty-two degrees, twenty-eight
minutes north of the last time
(circa 1997 CE)
i could make out the antipodes
upon whose bilateral peninsulas
my top-heavy preponderance poises
& eighty-seven degrees, four minutes,
nineteen-point-six seconds east of
Fuck You! Any more questions?

(Cento) Presentiment

I live, as the river does, in a mystery—
wedged in the middle of stars,
roses in bloom, penstemon,
the wet branches of an oak in winter—

where a small wind the size of a wrist pulls
the boaters in and makes the fish rise up,
like laughter that has found a final, silent
shape on a black sky wakes the cold.

See what the dark eats other than your heart:
That long shadow on the lawn will abide.
Death has a lot of time.

Stroke your strings. Listen to Vivaldi.
Then, as smoke you will rise to touch the sky,
dig a grave in the breezes.

Credits: Emily Dickinson, Louise Glück, Brigit Pegeen Kelly, Carmen Giménez-Smith, Larry Levis, Gwendolyn Brooks, C. D. Wright, Paul Celan (translated by Michael Hamburger)

The Corpus Callosum Is Unremarkable

—An In-titled Poem

. . . or, rather, there are no
lesions there, unlike in
other, special areas
(a.k.a., the temporal or
parietal lobes), so this
note isn't meant in particular
to be an insult . . .
Still, the MRI result's
essential premise misses
the entire point about
his brain: thus, it's not
a small slap to his persona,
nor to mine . . . Isn't it
much more than passable
to claim the real import
is lost to the meta-stases
cancer buries beneath
some lame, impenetrable
barrier to keep its cruelest
phases in a mausoleum?
So, let me at least issue
to the report this one
correction: because he *is*—
I mean, *all his parts are—
remarkable in-carnate!*
Oh, but he enamors me!
He completes me! He is—
it's simple, I'll spell it—
P— E— R— P— H— E— C— T !

Ghazal sans Answers

In brisk summer inquests, the willow tree answers:
Here, at the water's edge, I oversee answers.

His oncologist's Harvard sweatshirt signifies:
Medical Prodigy (though, minus the answers).

From the body-snatchers' dystopian clutches,
my dream-self cries: *Disco!* But nobody answers.

Our yowling tortoiseshell-tabby is spring-loaded
to waylay the first chump who faithfully answers.

If only Chuck's fealty to YouTube endorsements
of horse de-worming paste could guarantee answers . . .

I keen before the mother of fortune, a child
beseeching miracles . . . Necessity answers.

How to Squeeze Blood from a Turnip

—An In-titled Poem

Start with a seed in the dirt.

Water it but don't let it molder.

Wait for it to send a shoot up.

Draw near, then, to this new life form
and loom as a moth flutters about a flame.

Be alert, now, for, soon—
        as in, *quite soon,*
or to put it in plainer terms
for the fans tuned in at home,
before
the earthworm's first turn
toward the rain's warmth ends
with a sun-burnt twist;
for that matter,
before
our brown imp of a squirmer,
burrowed in its flower-bed, has earned
the most honest of dirt-naps as a robust
robin on the prowl's mid-strut meal;
before,
to be sure,
a sole salt-water fish,
rife with its hormonal flush
of hope, runs up-stream to spawn;

before
the nearest feudal lord dooms another serf
without a trial to be stoned to death,
but not until
after
he plows the potato field;
in other words,
sooner
than one would presume—
          our prized winter root,
transformed from a pint-sized sprout
to an entire, mature tuber, replete, now,
with a faint blush beneath its pate of lush flora,
is wont to burst top-first out of the soil, as if
to dispel our least doubt in this wonder—
     this promise of sweet
and bitter wealth—
          to be found
in the pith of buried flesh.

Behold, and reap what has been sown!

Feast!

Baby Robins

Having amassed five days
shell-less & blind
in the front-porch holly bush
the four siblings fattened;

four tongues budded
from the inchoate
darkness deep inside
four diaphanous necks

tussling atop peach-fuzzed torsos
teetering
as if disembodied
at the over-full nest's rim:

Having earned my five days
as *bird-nuisance-supreme*
of fly-bys & shrill scoldings
i was more than keen

for the inevitable tumbles
& rasping barks of parents frantic
for their unruly bundles' safe return
which (of course) i delivered—

but not before i took
those two exquisite dollops
of feather-dust-slick warmth
pulsing in fast-forward

into my crop's ripe darkness
where i keep
their bread-dough bellies
respiring

as i hush them to sleep . . .

The Final Frontier

I can't help that this word—
              with its bracing long ā—
never fails to evoke
the manifestly Shakespearean
monosyllable delivered by Jean Luc Picard:

"*Space: . . .*" ——   *Cake . . .*

See what I mean?

Could *that* have anything to do, I wonder,
with the way, every time I replace the word
for "Cake (with a big C)" with the word, *cake,*
you're now scrunching up your face as if you
mistakenly sucked on a lemon?

I hope it hasn't seemed to you, anyway,
like I wasn't taking your cake seriously,
when the truth is—
        & I need you to know it—
I've never taken anything more seriously
than the fact that you have cake:

    —that you're already sick & might yet
have a great deal more suffering to go, before,
regardless, you ultimately leave me—
        & what, if any, sliver of me
that could be left when you're gone would be
enough to keep on?

    —that I'm devastated unspeakably;

>   —because all I am and all I will
> ever be and cherish being is *Our WE—*
> >   this *sacred Infinite WE are—*
> that's now leading us into the unknown reaches
>
> of *Cake* . . .

By the Moonlit Water Where the *Dombiki* Sing

—An In-titled Poem

Elms looming ghostly
at the trail's stark edge;
the bower grows balmier
in midnight's mist;
and as a moonbeam
alights on a toadstool
newly bloating
in the dew-soaked loam,
i wend my way down
into that honey-dank glade
where, on a bygone night,
time's stealing-by steered
the moon in its sky,
while we held one another
and together we listened
to the *dombiki* sing . . .
      i learned, in that moment—
whether one wooed one,
or bolder twos wooed threes,
with their loose-stringed twangs
that mingled into tender harmonies—
      there was no way better
to be who we were together,
than beside the moonlit water
teeming with northern greens,
swathed in *dombiki*-ardor's song . . .
      and i gained a notion keener
that, too soon, i'd need to know:

Neither is there any better way to be alone—

Notes

The *In-titled Poem,* a poetry form invented by Stephanie L. Harper, is composed exclusively of the letters appearing in the poem's title, with no letter occurring within any single word in the poem more times than it does in its title. The following poems (listed in order of appearance) in *We Have Seen the Corn* are *In-titled Poems:*

"Pelvic Organ Prolapse"
"How to Squeeze Blood from a Turnip"
"The Corpus Callosum Is Unremarkable"
"By the Moonlit Water Where the *Dombiki* Sing"

About the Author

Stephanie L. Harper is a neurodivergent poet, mother, and transplant from Oregon now living in Indiana with the world's most adorable husband, son, cat, and puppy. In a former life, she earned her BA in English and German from Grinnell College, IA, and MA in German from the University of Wisconsin-Madison.

More recently, she homeschooled and raised her extraordinary son and daughter to adulthood in Oregon and completed her MFA in Poetry at Butler University in Indianapolis, IN. Her poems appear in *Crab Creek Review, The Iowa Review, Laurel Review, The Night Heron Barks, North Dakota Quarterly, Panoply, Pleiades, Salamander Magazine, Slippery Elm Literary Journal, Taos Journal of Poetry,* and elsewhere.

www.ingramcontent.com/pod-product-compliance
Lightning Source LLC
Chambersburg PA
CBHW030917170426
43193CB00009BA/886